10

T0182254

100%
UNOFFICIAL

First published in Great Britain 2024 by 100% Unofficial, a part of Farshore
An imprint of HarperCollins*Publishers*
1 London Bridge Street, London SE1 9GF
www.farshore.co.uk

HarperCollins*Publishers*
Macken House, 39/40 Mayor Street Upper,
Dublin 1, D01 C9W8, Ireland

Written by Ben Wilson

This book is an original creation by Farshore
© 2024 HarperCollins*Publishers* Limited

Additional imagery used under license from Shutterstock.com

ISBN 978 0 00 870832 0
Printed in Malaysia
001

A CIP catalogue record for this title is available from the British Library.

Stay safe online. Farshore is not responsible for content hosted by third parties.

This book contains FSC™ certified paper and other controlled sources to ensure responsible forest management.

For more information visit: www.harpercollins.co.uk/green

TAYLOR SWIFT

GUIDE

CONTENTS

08 IT'S ME, HI!

10 TAYLOR TIMELINE

12 BORN IN THE U.S.TAY

14 ALBUM SPOTLIGHT: TAYLOR SWIFT

16 13 ... BEST SHOWS AND ALBUMS

18 TOTALLY TAYLOR: RAINBOW FASHION

20 ALBUM SPOTLIGHT: FEARLESS

22 13 ... BEST AWARDS

24 TOTALLY TAYLOR: FASHION FORWARD

26 ALBUM SPOTLIGHT: SPEAK NOW

28 13 ... BILLBOARD HOT 100 HITS

30 TOTALLY TAYLOR: WITH THE GOOD HAIR

32 ALBUM SPOTLIGHT: RED

34 TOTALLY TAYLOR: WISE WORDS

36 TOTALLY TAYLOR: FAMOUS FRIENDS

38 ALBUM SPOTLIGHT: 1989

40   **13 ... TOP COLLABORATIONS**

42   **ALBUM SPOTLIGHT: REPUTATION**

44   **TOTALLY TAYLOR: AT HOME WITH TAYLOR**

46   **ALBUM SPOTLIGHT: LOVER**

48   **TOTALLY TAYLOR: CAT CREW**

50   **13 ... CRAZIEST HEADLINES**

52   **ALBUM SPOTLIGHT: FOLKLORE**

54   **TOTALLY TAYLOR: I ♥ T.S**

56   **ALBUM SPOTLIGHT: EVERMORE**

58   **TOTALLY TAYLOR: COOLEST CONCERTS**

60   **13 ... BEST MUSIC VIDEOS**

62   **ALBUM SPOTLIGHT: MIDNIGHTS**

64   **13 ... BEST VIDEO CAMEOS**

66   **TOTALLY TAYLOR: ONE DAY ON THE ERAS TOUR**

68   **ALBUM SPOTLIGHT: THE TORTURED POETS DEPARTMENT**

IT'S ME, HI!
TAYLOR SWIFT

Wanna know Tay-Tay all too well? Memorise these fabulous facts!

NAME:

Taylor Alison Swift

BIRTHDAY:

13 December 1989

STAR SIGN:

Sagittarius, which usually means passionate, charming and intelligent. That's our Tay!

BORN:

West Reading, Pennsylvania, USA

HEIGHT:

1.80m

TV:

Taylor's all-time top show is *Gilmore Girls*. She also loves *Friends*, *Game of Thrones*, *Grey's Anatomy* and *Downton Abbey*.

Taylor bossing it in a glitzy gold dress at a screening of *All Too Well: The Short Film* at the 2022 Toronto Film Festival.

FAVOURITE COLOUR:

Loving her is red, but in an interview with Ellen DeGeneres when she was younger, Taylor said **her fave colour is actually purple.**

MOVIE:

1980s classics **The Breakfast Club** and **Sixteen Candles**, and period drama **Sense & Sensibility**, are big Taylor loves – and she adores the **Barbie** movie.

BOOK:

The song 'Tolerate It' was inspired by **Daphne du Maurier's Rebecca**, which was written in 1938! Taylor also loves the *Harry Potter* and *Hunger Games* series.

INFLUENCES:

Shania Twain, The Chicks, Joni Mitchell, Paul McCartney and – of course! – **Tim McGraw**.

ANIMALS:

Her **three cats** are now legendary. They're called **Meredith Grey**, **Olivia Benson** and **Benjamin Button**!

GAMES:

When on tour, Taylor loves to play a round of **Scrabble** with her mum!

ROLE MODEL:

Taylor once named actress **Mariska Hargitay** as her role model. Things came full circle a decade later when Mariska named her cat Karma!

FOOD:

Buckwheat crepes for breakfast, hummus as a snack and chicken fajitas or cauliflower casserole at dinner time!

NUMBER:

13, it's her **birth date**, she turned 13 on Friday 13th and her first album went gold in 13 weeks!

DRINKS:

A grande caramel non-fat latte!

CHARITY:

She's one of the **most generous** celebs, famed for paying off fans' student loans and pledging $1 million to flood relief efforts.

Taylor often scrawls "13" on her hand for good luck – and her X account is @taylorswift13!

9

TAYLOR TIMELINE

All the important dates in Taylor's life so far ...

Forever and always the belle of the ball at the 2008 Grammy Awards.

1989

Taylor Alison Swift is born on **13 December** in Reading, Pennsylvania, to dad Scott and mum Andrea.

2002

Taylor performs **'The Star-Spangled Banner'** during a Philadelphia 76ers basketball game. She's just **eleven years old**! Around this time she also writes her first song, **'Lucky You'**, after a computer repair man shows her how to play three chords: C, D and G.

2008

Second album *Fearless* begins T-Swift's crossover from country to pop. **'Love Story'** and **'You Belong With Me'** become two of her signature songs. It soon claims the **Album of the Year Grammy**. Once the album is out, Taylor begins preparations for her first ever live tour.

| 1989 | 2002 | 2006 | 2008 | 2010 | 2012 |

Tim McGraw isn't just a song name. He's also a country icon who's made 16 albums!

2010

Taylor spends the first half of the year finishing the **Fearless Tour**, playing **118 shows** in total. **'Mine'** is released as the debut single from third album *Speak Now* – with every song penned by Taylor all on her own.

2006

First single **'Tim McGraw'** jumps straight onto the USA's Billboard chart and stays there for eight months! It's followed up by her **debut album**, called *Taylor Swift*. Standout tracks include **'Our Song'** and **'Teardrops On My Guitar'**.

Taylor having the best day on stage at Madison Square Garden, New York, during the Fearless Tour.

2012

Taylor claims a world record! **'We Are Never Ever Getting Back Together'** tops the iTunes Chart, 50 minutes after release, making it the **fastest selling single ever**. It's her first number one single. Fourth album *Red* is just as huge, selling 1.2 million copies in one week!

2019

Taylor's seventh album is her most romantic yet. *Lover* is all about being bright, bold and free, with tracks like **'The Man'** and **'You Need To Calm Down'** promoting equality. Fans are surprised, however, when the catchy **'Cruel Summer'** isn't released as a single.

2017

After nearly a year out of the spotlight, Taylor returns with sixth album *Reputation*. Fans are invited for secret listening sessions before its release, as lead single **'Look What You Made Me Do'** answers her critics. So great to have her back!

Our girl smashing it as usual on the Eras Tour. How many times have you watched the movie?!

2023

Taylor's biggest year yet. The **Eras Tour** sees her play **44 songs over three and a half hours** and is acclaimed as the greatest pop show in history! She earns 9 wins at the MTV Video Music Awards, becomes a billionaire and is named **Person of the Year** by *Time* magazine!

| 2014 | 2017 | 2019 | 2020 | 2022 | 2023 | 2024 |

Shaking it off on the 1989 Tour!

2020

We get two Swift albums in one year! Holed up with her cats because of the pandemic, Taylor records *Folklore* and *Evermore* remotely. Their laid-back feel earns rave reviews, with **'Illicit Affairs'** and **'Champagne Problems'** becoming fan faves.

2022

Taylor announces the track names for tenth album *Midnights* on social media, using bingo balls! Everyone loves first single **'Anti-Hero'** which goes deep on electronics and drum machine beats, again reinventing our favourite lady.

2024

Thanks to *Midnights*, T-Swift becomes the first artist in Grammys history to win **Album of the Year** four times. She celebrates by announcing album eleven: *The Tortured Poets Department*!

2014

Tay-Tay makes her **first official pop album** and names it after her birth year: *1989*. **'Shake It Off'** goes supermassive across the globe, even inspiring a lip-synced version from Dwayne 'The Rock' Johnson! **'Blank Space'** and **'Style'** are mega hits too.

Taylor performed at the December 2019 Jingle Bell Ball, just before the pandemic hit.

BORN IN THE U.S.TAY!

America loves its biggest pop star! Here's a map of all the major stops on Taylor's journey to the top ...

GLENDALE, ARIZONA

The phenomenal **Eras Tour** kicked off here on 17 March 2023. It was the first of **151 shows** over five continents, and gave us a flavour of what to expect – like two different **surprise songs** every evening! The first were 'Tim McGraw' and 'Mirrorball'.

The Eras Tour trucked all across America – then south to Mexico, Brazil and beyond!

TAYLOR SWIFT EDUCATION CENTER

NASHVILLE, TENNESSEE

The centre of the Taylor Swift universe. These days it even has a **Taylor Swift Education Center**. You can go there to see her wardrobe, guitars and behind-the-scenes photos from the making of *Speak Now*!

LOS ANGELES, CALIFORNIA

The final Eras Tour dates in Taylor's homeland took her to SoFi Stadium, for six nights! All-sister group **Haim** were her support act and returned halfway through Tay's set to duet on 'No Body, No Crime'!

HENDERSONVILLE, TENNESSEE

Nashville is known as the home of **country music**, so Taylor's family moved to nearby Hendersonville when she was 14. She then played loads of **local shows** during her teenage years to build up a dedicated fanbase. It worked!

READING, PENNSYLVANIA

Taylor Alison Swift was **born here** on **13 December 1989**. It's a city with a population of 95,000, and they're very proud of their hometown girl!

BROOKLYN, NEW YORK

"From where your Brooklyn broke my skin and bones …" If you love that incredible lyric from **'All Too Well (10 Minute Version)'**, this needs no further explanation!

WATCH HILL, RHODE ISLAND

Tay paid more than $17 million to buy a house here in 2013. She loves the area so much it inspired *Evermore* track **'The Last Great American Dynasty'**. The song is about Rebekah Harkness, who Taylor bought the house from!

WYOMISSING, PENNSYLVANIA

Taylor grew up here with her parents and younger brother Austin. Her home was a **Christmas tree farm** and it inspired the song of the same name!

STONE HARBOR, NEW JERSEY

Taylor used to **holiday** here in the summer as a teenager, performing in a **local coffee shop**!

NEW YORK, NEW YORK

Taylor moved to the Big Apple in March 2014 and began putting together her fifth album, *1989*. Now you know why she called the very first track **'Welcome To New York'**! **'Cornelia Street'** is also named after a place where Tay once lived.

ARLINGTON, TEXAS

When the Eras Tour arrived here Taylor was awarded with a **key to the city**. And a local street called Randol Mill Road temporarily had its name changed to **Taylor Swift Way**!

THE MARSHES, NORTH CAROLINA

The setting for one of Taylor's saddest songs: **'Carolina'**, from the soundtrack to movie *Where The Crawdads Sing*.

Taylor rocked Times Square with 'I Knew You Were Trouble' on NYE 2013!

TAYLOR SWIFT

COUNTRY BEGINNINGS

Taylor was just 16 when her first album came out in October 2006. It only sold 40,000 copies in its first week, but word of its brilliance slowly spread. A year later, sales passed the one million mark! The album focussed on the teenage experiences of growing up in a small American town, with a strong country music vibe.

Those colossal curls are a legendary memory of the *Taylor Swift* era.

TIED TOGETHER WITH A SMILE

Taylor had been writing songs for four years by the time her album came out. That made for a clever mix of thought-provoking themes! **'Tim McGraw'** is about hoping a boyfriend won't forget her when he leaves for college. **'Picture To Burn'** is a heartbreak song, while **'The Outside'** was written when she was twelve and is about Taylor's friends shunning her because she loved country music. She definitely had the last laugh!

HIGH SCHOOL MUSICAL

The album's success meant that Taylor finished 2007 as the **tenth biggest selling artist of the year**, despite only just having graduated from high school!

OUR SONG = YOUR SONG

In a Billboard poll, fans voted **'Our Song'** as the best song on the album. It scored **19% of the vote**, just ahead of **'Teardrops On My Guitar'** and **'Picture To Burn'**.

BEST MATHS LESSON EVER

'Tim McGraw' was Taylor's first ever single. She wrote it in a maths class at school! It came out in June 2006 and **reached number 40** in the US charts. The vinyl edition is so rare, it's now worth around £400!

ODD ONE OUT

Taylor's first album is the only one that doesn't have its own section in the Eras Tour. However, a **'secret song'** performance of **'Our Song'** does appear in the **movie**. And those who attended the first night of the tour in Arizona were rewarded with a one-off **'Tim McGraw'** singalong!

BAD LUCK, BOYS!

"Most of the songs on the album are **about actual people** that have been in my life," Taylor told *Entertainment Weekly*. For instance, **'Teardrops On My Guitar'** is about a boy called Drew, while another potential love interest named Corey inspired **'Stay Beautiful'**. Imagine being those guys now, and discovering you missed out on dating Taylor Swift!

Shortly after the release of *Taylor Swift*, she collaborated with veteran UK rockers Def Leppard for CMT Crossroads. Seek out their duet on 'When Love & Hate Collide'!

13 ... BEST SHOWS AND ALBUMS

It's almost impossible to narrow the top gigs and records of Tay's career down to 13. But here's a gutsy attempt!

1

ME AND MY GANG TOUR

Tay wasn't famous enough to promote the *Taylor Swift* album with her own tour. Instead, she supported country group **Rascal Flats**. Tay only played five tracks, including **'Our Song'**, but those present knew they were watching a **future megastar**!

2

FEARLESS

Taylor's second album is the one that made her a superstar. *Fearless* went to **number one** in the USA, Australia, Ireland and New Zealand in 2008 – then did the same again when re-released as *Taylor's Version* 13 years later!

3

REPUTATION STADIUM TOUR

Some **critics doubted** the *Reputation* album when it was released, but this huge tour made them think again. Finally, the world saw just how good songs like **'Look What You Made Me Do'** and **'...Ready For It?'** really were.

The Fearless Tour spanned 118 dates and even had its own DVD and Blu-Ray, called *Journey to Fearless*.

4

LOVER

Netflix documentary *Miss Americana* tracked Taylor's mission to make an **album that celebrated love**, instead of being about heartbreak! *Lover* was the result and track **'Cruel Summer'** is now a **TikTok phenomenon**.

5

FEARLESS TOUR

Miss Swift's first ever **headline tour** took her across North America and included two dates in the UK. It was mainly songs from her first two albums – but she surprised her LA fans by performing **'Hot N Cold'** with Katy Perry!

FOLKLORE

6

TayTay **stunned the world** in July 2020, when, midway through the pandemic, she released this low-key wonder. Not only that, follow-up *Evermore* dropped just five months later!

V FESTIVAL 2009

7

Taylor's **first UK festival** appearance came in Chelmsford, and she wasn't even the headliner! Instead, that honour went to The Killers. Still, Tay **knocked it out of the park** with hits like '**Love Story**' and '**You Belong With Me**'.

Taylor rocking V Festival in 2009. Other highlights across the weekend included Calvin Harris, Lily Allen and Lady Gaga!

1989

8

So good it brought us two different sets of Swift insta-classics: '**Blank Space**' and '**Shake It Off**' when the original came out in 2014, then '**Is It Over Now?**' and '**Say Don't Go**' on the 2023 *Taylor's Version*!

CITY OF LOVER

9

For one night only, Taylor dropped into **Paris** to promote her seventh album, *Lover*. You could only get a ticket by winning an **online contest** after buying the album! It was the first time she'd ever played '**Death By A Thousand Cuts**', '**Cornelia Street**' and '**The Man**' live.

10 ## MIDNIGHTS

Did you meet her at midnight? If so, the reward was bangers like '**Lavender Haze**', '**Anti-Hero**' and '**Bejeweled**'. Best believe it's **iconic**.

11 ## THE 1989 WORLD TOUR

T-Swift's fourth tour took seven months to plan, and three more to rehearse! Most nights saw her perform with a **one-off special guest**. They included Lorde, Ed Sheeran and Imagine Dragons!

RED

12

Taylor **slayed** here with tunes like '**We Are Never Ever Getting Back Together**' and '**I Knew You Were Trouble**'. It was so consistent that fan favourite '**All Too Well**' wasn't even released as a single!

THE ERAS TOUR

13

The **greatest music show** by any artist, ever. It features **44 songs** from all her past albums, performed over a mammoth three-and-half hours. Perfection.

TOTALLY TAYLOR: RAINBOW FASHION

Taylor loves including colours in her lyrics and is also considered an LGBTQ+ icon. So naturally she looks spectacular in every colour of the rainbow!

BURNING RED

Of course T-Swift looks amazing in red – she did, after all, name an entire album after that colour! This is her looking extra glam while being proclaimed **Woman of the Year** at the 2012 Billboard Music Awards.

ORANGE PREMIERE

Orange was the theme of the world premiere for animated movie *Dr Seuss' The Lorax*, in which Taylor played Zac Efron's love interest Audrey. To fit in, she chose an elegant yet understated dress.

CANARY YELLOW

Is there anyone on the planet who carries off yellow better than Tay-Tay? Nope! Look closely and you'll see her friend Lorde in the background of this trip to the **Golden Globes**.

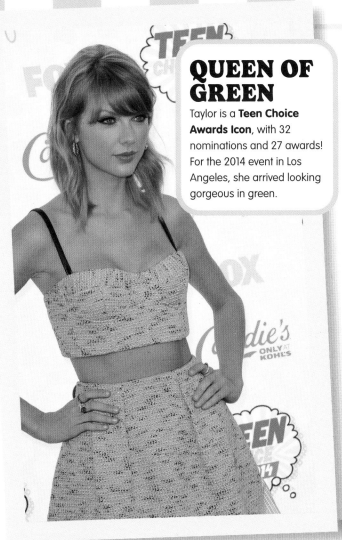

QUEEN OF GREEN

Taylor is a **Teen Choice Awards Icon**, with 32 nominations and 27 awards! For the 2014 event in Los Angeles, she arrived looking gorgeous in green.

IT'S BLUE!

Baby blue was the order of the day when Taylor rocked up at the **MTV Video Music Awards** during the *Red* era. Both paparazzi and fans were stunned by her killer of a romper suit!

INDIGO EYES

Our girl looked beautiful in indigo at the **Billboard Music Awards** in 2013. Her outfit got even better with the addition of some gold: eight awards, including top artist and top album!

LOVELY IN VIOLET

Taylor's first appearance at the **Grammy Awards** was as graceful as her Eras Tour performances of **'Enchanted'** over a decade later. She wore a strapless silk Sandy Spika gown, but missed out to Amy Winehouse as Best New Artist.

FEARLESS

TAYLOR'S FIRST GRAMMY

There's no greater trophy in music than a Grammy Award. *Fearless* came out in November 2008 and saw Taylor take home the prize for Album Of The Year! She was the youngest winner of all time. Her second album spent 11 weeks at the top of the US charts and over the years its sales have risen to over 12 million!

TayTay wowed the crowds during the Fearless Tour, with hits like 'Change' and 'Fifteen'!

A HEFTY CATALOGUE

Title track **'Fearless'** was the first song Taylor penned for the album. Even though Tay was officially famous, she still wanted the record to be **personal and relatable**, and that track was about an imaginary first date. In the end she wrote **75 songs**, which had to be knocked down to a track-list of 13!

SHAKESPEAREAN TALE

'Love Story' came out two months before the album itself. "I wrote [it] on my bedroom floor, in about 20 minutes!" Taylor told *Time* magazine. It was inspired by **Shakespeare's play** *Romeo and Juliet*, and fans lapped it up. It sold **18 million copies**, while the music video is utterly iconic!

TROPHY HAUL

Fearless has won more awards than any country album in history! As well as the main **Album of the Year Grammy**, it was also **Country Album of the Year** at the prestigious show. The Country Music Association and Academy of Country Music also named it their **Album of the Year**.

MUSICAL FRIEND

Fourth track **'Hey Stephen'** is addressed to a real person! He's called **Stephen Barker Liles** and is in a group called **Love and Theft**. To say thanks, he wrote Taylor a lovely song called **'Try To Make It Anyway'**!

THE FIRST TAYLOR'S VERSION

After the release of *Lover*, Taylor's boss sold off the rights to her first six albums. Boooo! Her response was to re-record them all, and *Fearless (Taylor's Version)* came out first, in 2021. Seven brand new **'From The Vault'** tracks included **'That's When'**, alongside country legend Keith Urban!

JUMP THEN FALL

Taylor wrote **'Fifteen'** about her best friend at the time, Abigail Anderson, and their **troubles with boys**. Both had their hearts broken while in high school and she wanted to get across the feelings and hurt they shared!

(ALMOST) TOP OF THE POPS

'Fearless', **'Love Story'**, **'You Belong With Me'**, **'Change'** and **'Jump Then Fall'** all made it into the **USA top 10** – but none got to number one!

The 2008 MTV Music Video Awards took place shortly before the release of *Fearless*. Taylor earned a best new artist nomination for 'Teardrops On My Guitar'!

VIDEO MUSIC AWARD HOLLYWOOD 2008

VIDEO MUSIC AWAR 2008 HOLLYWOO

13 ... BEST AWARDS

Taylor needs multiple homes to hold her collection of gold! These are a few of the awards she's gained ...

The 2010 Grammys were legendary for Tay. Here she is posing with all four of her remarkable awards!

1

ALBUM OF THE YEAR

Only one artist in history has won this esteemed Grammy **four different times**. It's Taylor, or course! She nabbed it for *Fearless* in 2010, *1989* in 2016, *Folklore* in 2021 and *Midnights* in 2024.

2

AMERICAN MUSIC AWARDS

This star-studded show began in 1973. Taylor has picked up **40 separate AMA wins** in her career – 14 more than Michael Jackson, in second place!

3

BRIT AWARDS

UK experts have been tougher on Tay-Tay than those across the pond. She only has **two Brits** so far, although one is a **Global Icon Award**. Phew!

4

FOUR GRAMMYS IN ONE GO

One of the most famous Taylor photos is from the **2010 Grammy Awards**. She's holding two trophies for the *Fearless* album and another two for the song **'White Horse'**!

5

MOST CHART ENTRIES

Taylor's first world record, in 2008, was for the **most USA chart entries in a single year** (six). She now holds **118 world records** in total!

6

GREATEST SEISMIC ACTIVITY

T-Swift scored a **Guinness World Record** when the Eras Tour came to Seattle. Fans danced and cheered so crazily, it felt like a **2.3 magnitude earthquake**!

7
HIGHEST-GROSSING MUSIC TOUR

The **Eras Tour** has picked up a ton of awards and world records. It's made more money than any tour in history – and the **movie** is the highest-grossing concert film ever!

HONORARY DEGREE

New York University awarded Taylor an honorary degree in 2022. It's a **Doctorate of Fine Arts**!

8

Taylor was overjoyed to collect her honorary degree, blowing kisses to a delighted Yankee Stadium crowd.

9
MTV VIDEO OF THE YEAR

Taylor is known for her **knockout pop vids**. Naturally, she's claimed this award four times: for **'Bad Blood'**, **'You Need To Calm Down'**, **'All Too Well'** and **'Anti-Hero'**.

10
PERSON OF THE YEAR

The world-famous *Time* **magazine** gives this award out every December to the individual who "has done the most to influence the events of the year". After the Eras Tour helped Taylor become the **planet's biggest pop star**, she was named Person of the Year for 2023!

11
TAYLOR SWIFT AWARD

Broadcast Music, Inc celebrated Tay's greatness by giving her … The Taylor Swift award! Only **Michael Jackson** had received the honour before. "If they had chosen someone else to give the Taylor Swift Award to, I'd be kind of bummed about it," she told the audience!

WOMAN OF THE DECADE

Billboard proclaimed Taylor the **greatest woman of the 2010s**! It was a decade where she released five albums, fought back against her music being sold off and restored her reputation – which is where that album title comes from!

12

AMERICAN COUNTRY MUSIC VIDEO OF THE YEAR

You might not know the first Taylor song to score an award! **'Highway Don't Care'** was made with Tim McGraw and Keith Urban, and picked up the **ACM Video of the Year** award in 2014.

13

TOTALLY TAYLOR: FASHION FORWARD

Taylor isn't afraid to go out of style with unique outfits and unexpected looks. These are some of her most memorable fits!

BLEACH LIFE

The theme was 'Manus x Machina' when Tay co-hosted the **Met Gala fashion show**, so she wore a metallic Louis Vuitton dress and boots. Dark lipstick and a new bleach-blonde bob completed the jaw-dropping look.

LOOK WHAT YOU MADE HER DO

The **2018 American Music Awards** saw Tay sport the most incredible outfit of her career. Designed by Olivier Roustieng, Taylor paired a shiny silver Balmain minidress worth $7,650 with thigh-high boots. Oh, and a snake ring, to celebrate **Reputation**!

PYJAMA PARTY

You'd be forgiven for thinking that Taylor was in her PJs for this night out at the **MTV Music Awards**! Her two-piece outfit by Ashish proved that she looks great even in a crop top and joggers!

FLOWER GIRL

What a year 2020 was for Taylor, with the release of both *Folklore* and *Evermore*. Little could we have known that they were coming when she arrived at the **Golden Globes** in February. This teal and yellow Etro dress, accessorised with Lorraine Schwartz jewellery, was one of her most startling looks ever!

RULE BRI-TAY-NNIA

Wow! Taylor kicked off the 2013 **Victoria's Secret Fashion Show** in this eye-popping Union Jack outfit. She performed '**I Knew You Were Trouble**' in the flag-print mini-dress, one-armed blazer and tiny top hat. No wonder she'd one day fall for a London boy!

TRAIL BLAZER

Taylor went bold with this multicoloured blazer dress at the 2019 **MTV Video Music Awards**. She paired the Versace blazer with super high, over-the-knee Louboutin boots.

SPEAK NOW

ENCHANTED TO MEET YOU

No collaborators, no co-writers: Taylor penned her entire third album without any help whatsoever. Genius! It's mainly focussed on love, heartbreak and healing, and was more grown up than the teenage experiences of her first two albums. The world adored it and it sold one million copies in its first week on sale.

TS performing in Speak Now purple at the NBC Today Show in New York.

SIX SINGLES

The song **'Enchanted'** is a pillar of the Eras Tour, with dancers twirling around Taylor in her **ballgown**. But it was never released as a single! Instead, the songs chosen to represent *Speak Now* were **'Mine'**, **'Back To December'**, **'Mean'**, **'The Story Of Us'**, **'Sparks Fly'** and **'Ours'**.

THIS NIGHT IS SPARKLIN'

Most of the songs for *Speak Now* were written on the road, during the Fearless Tour! The album came out in October 2010, two months before Taylor's **21st birthday**. She spent the big day recording at a Nashville studio!

> "I'd get my best ideas at 3 a.m. in Arkansas and I didn't have a co-writer around so I would just finish it."
>
> *Taylor explained this in a 2010 interview with Songwriter Universe.*

A TAY APOLOGY

Taylor says **'Back To December'** is the first time she's ever apologised to someone in a song. For years, fans suspected it was about **Taylor Lautner**, who Swift dated in 2009. Lautner since confirmed it was indeed about him and that the pair remained on friendly terms!

BACK TO THE FUTURE

'Sparks Fly' is one of *Speak Now*'s signature tracks, but was actually an oldie! Taylor **wrote it before the release of her first album**. Fans heard the track when footage of an early concert appeared on the internet and begged her to record a proper version. So she did!

HITS DIFFERENT

As well as being a top track, **'Enchanted'** was the **original name for the album**! However, Taylor's record company boss felt that it didn't fit with the mature songwriting on show. So Taylor chose *Speak Now*, feeling it was a good **motto for life**!

STARS ALIGN

Taylor did let some collaborators join her when recording the updated *Taylor's Version*. She duetted with **Fallout Boy** on **'Electric Touch'** and **Hayley Williams from Paramore** on **'Castles Crumbling'**!

The Speak Now Tour ran for over a year! It kicked off in February 2011, and ran until March 2012 – with 110 shows in total.

13 ... BILLBOARD HOT 100 HITS

Taylor has been busy creating 'sick beats' since day one, so let's take a look at her top 13 Billboard Hot 100 hits ...

Taylor kicked off her Speak Now Tour in 2011 in Fort Lauderdale, Florida. That lucky 13 on her hand must have worked as her show sold out in every single country!

1 SHAKE IT OFF

Of course the iconic **'Shake It Off'** is Swift's **biggest charting single**! The song debuted at number one in the Hot 100 and spent four weeks at the top. It stayed in the Hot 100 for almost **six months**!

2 ANTI-HERO

It's me, hi ... I'm the second bestselling Tay-Tay single; it's me. The hit stayed in the number one spot for **six weeks in a row**.

3 YOU BELONG WITH ME

You OK? Good, because this beat hit the number two spot in 2009, becoming the **first country song to top the all-genre Radio Songs chart**. Oh, and don't forget that classic music video – get your notebooks out!

4 BLANK SPACE

Who did Swift replace at the number one spot with **'Blank Space'**? Herself! She **removed 'Shake It Off' from the top spot** and filled that blank space with her own name again.

5 LOVE STORY

An oldie but a goldie. The lead single from *Fearless* hit the **number four spot**, just behind **'You Belong With Me'**. If you love romantic, fairy tale magic, just say "yes".

6 CRUEL SUMMER

Although '**Cruel Summer**' didn't top the charts when Taylor's *Lover* album was first released, it finally made it **four years later**, reaching number one in October 2023.

7 I KNEW YOU WERE TROUBLE

Taylor's self-described 'chaotic' hit debuted at number three in the Hot 100, eventually reaching **number two**. No screaming goats here!

8 WE ARE NEVER EVER GETTING BACK TOGETHER

Tay-Tay's first ever (like, ever) **Hot 100 number one** came in 2012 and stayed in the top spot for three weeks. The tune set the record for the **most digital sales of a song by a woman** – clearly there was no indie record that was *much* cooler than hers.

Rocking those sunnies! Taylor paired edgy white sunglasses with her colourful sequin look on her 1989 Tour.

9 BAD BLOOD FEAT. KENDRICK LAMAR

It's fiery. It's fierce. And it features an iconic girl squad ready to take anyone down. The legendary hit reached number one after the **action-packed music video** was released. The video also broke Vevo's viewing record, reaching **20.1 million global views** in its first 24 hours!

10 I DON'T WANNA LIVE FOREVER FEAT. ZAYN

Her first single following the success of *1989*, Swift **collaborated with Zayn from One Direction** in this romantic song, reaching number two in 2017.

11 WILDEST DREAMS

This heartfelt, dreamy song peaked at number five in 2015. To top it off, all of the proceeds from the music video, which was mostly filmed in Botswana, went to **wild animal conservation**, through the African Parks Foundation of America.

12 STYLE

Following her dazzling performance at the **Victoria's Secret Fashion Show** in 2014, '**Style**' entered the Hot 100, eventually reaching number six.

13 LOOK WHAT YOU MADE ME DO

I'm sorry, Taylor can't come to the phone right now … because she's too busy at number one again. The lead single from *Reputation* became **Taylor's fifth single to reach the top.**

TOTALLY TAYLOR: WITH THE GOOD HAIR

Taylor's music and videos have turned her into a fashion icon, meaning lots of new hairdos over the years. These are the best!

FAMOUS FIRST LOOK

Think of Taylor's early years and her **honey-blonde curls** will spring to mind. They made her instantly recognisable from Nashville to Newcastle and still look stunning in the vids for **'Fearless'** and **'You Belong With Me'**.

CRASH, BOOM, BANGS!

Early fans were initially shocked when Tay switched her look for the **2010 American Music Awards**. Out went the famous curls and in came impeccable straight **blonde bangs**. It took just one performance of **'Back To December'** to win everyone over!

CURLS UNFURLED

The **country curls** made a delightful return at the **2013 MTV Video Music Awards**, as Taylor claimed best vid for **'I Knew You Were Trouble'**.

LONG STORY SHORT

Taylor stunned the world at the **2016 Grammys**, rocking up with Selena Gomez and a new **bob hairstyle**. It proved a good omen. She won **Album of the Year** for *1989*!

BLEACH GETAWAY

Stunning! Taylor turned her hair **platinum blonde** to co-host the **2016 Met Gala**. Adding dark lipstick made her look especially badass. Fans still refer to this look as **Bleachella**!

CALL IT WHAT YOU WANT

The Reputation Tour saw Taylor adopt her **darkest, edgiest look yet**, with her longer hair matched by berry-coloured lipstick. Our girl had fully grown up, and yep – we were very ready for it!

RETRO LOVER

'Cruel Summer'? More like Cool Summer! The *Lover* era saw Tay change looks again, adopting this **1960s-themed half-up hairstyle**. She truly is the queen of reinvention.

RED

EVERYTHING HAS CHANGED

Taylor's fourth album was her most ambitious so far. She tried out a number of new co-writers and producers to add rockier, dancier elements to her country pop style. First single 'We Are Never Ever Getting Back Together' perfected this vision! Taylor chose the name *Red* as the colour summed up the emotions she felt while making the album.

Ed Sheeran came aboard to duet on 'Everything Has Changed', and has been great mates with Taylor ever since.

A PERFECT TEAM

Taylor loves to collaborate with different artists, and this time she teamed up with Brit favourite **Ed Sheeran** on **'Everything Has Changed'** and Snow Patrol frontman **Gary Lightbody** on **'The Last Time'**.

> **"I didn't choose [my co-writers] because I wanted to force my style on them; I chose them because I wanted to learn from them."**
>
> *Taylor told this to USA Today about the album's collaborations.*

STOCKHOLM CALLING

Swedish music god **Max Martin** worked with Taylor on the record and **co-wrote three songs**, including **'22'**. His other huge hits include 'Roar' by Katy Parry and Britney Spears' tune '…Baby One More Time'!

HITS, HITS, HITS

Red spawned **more singles** than any previous Taylor album: **seven**! They were **'We Are Never Ever Getting Back Together'**, **'Begin Again'**, **'I Knew You Were Trouble'**, **'22'**, **'Red'**, **'Everything Has Changed'** and **'The Last Time'**.

A YEAR IN THE MAKING

Taylor started writing the album in February 2011 and continued while **on the road** with the Speak Now Tour. By November she had 25 songs ready, with the album eventually emerging in **October 2012**.

ALL'S WELL THAT ENDS WELL

'All Too Well' was the first song written for the album. It never came out as a single, but fans loved it, particularly when Taylor mentioned that there was a secret extended demo! After years of pleading, it was finally added to *Red (Taylor's Version)* – and went straight to **number one**.

RAINBOW OF WORDS

While it might be called *Red*, the colours **blue, grey, green and black also feature** in the lyrics. And **silver**, if you count **'I Bet You Think About Me'** from *Red (Taylor's Version)*!

As well as a new feel to her music, *Red* also saw T-Swift switch her look. Out went her lush country curls and in came striking blonde bangs!

33

TOTALLY TAYLOR: WISE WORDS

As well as being the world's greatest modern songwriter, Taylor is known for her brilliant advice and life insights ...

"Did you ever watch the movie *Love Actually*, where Hugh Grant's voiceover says, 'If you look around, love actually is all around'? That's my favourite motto." Little wonder Taylor made an album called *Lover*, after sharing this insight with *Teen Vogue*!

The past, present and future are all things to be positive about. **"You should celebrate who you are now, where you're going, and where you've been,"** Taylor told *Time* magazine in 2023.

Across the globe, Taylor always strives to make time for her fans.

Taylor claimed Top Female Artist at the 2018 Billboard Music Awards – and stunned in this pink Versace gown.

Endings are an essential part of who we are. Before introducing *Sad Beautiful Tragic* at a 2013 live show, Taylor said this: **"Just because something is over doesn't mean it wasn't incredibly beautiful. 'Cause another lesson I've learned is that not all stories have a happy ending, and you have to learn how to deal with that."**

"A song can defy logic or time." Taylor opens up on why she feels lyrics and music are such a magical experience while collecting Songwriter-Artist of the Decade at the Nashville Songwriters Association International Awards in 2022.

TayTay believes that personal drive and ambition propel you on the journey through life. **"You are the only one who gets to decide what you will be remembered for,"** she wrote in the album notes for *1989*.

T-Swift claimed four 2009 Country Music Association Awards, including Album of the Year and Female Vocalist of the Year.

The Lover deluxe editions featured four journals with revealing and inspiring insights into Tay's life, such as this: **"Don't ever let anyone make you think that you don't deserve what you want."**

"Life is short. Have adventures." Naturally, Taylor had some incredible advice on how we can all enjoy our day-to-day existence more when she was named *Time* Person of the Year in 2023.

Fearless wasn't just an album title, but a way Taylor wanted to approach her craft as fame came calling. **"To me, fearless is living in spite of those things that scare you to death,"** she wrote in the album notes.

"It's good to mess up and learn from it and take risks." Nobody is perfect, not even Taylor Swift! This amazing life advice came during an *Elle* interview in 2019.

Of course our girl won video of the year for 'All Too Well (10 Minute Version) (Taylor's Version)' at the 2022 MTV Video Music Awards.

TOTALLY TAYLOR: FAMOUS FRIENDS

From the famed Girl Squad to her teenage bestie, these are the go-to pals in Taylor's world ...

HAIM

Along with going pop, fifth album *1989* saw the emergence of Taylor's **Girl Squad**. These celebrity queens would often be seen with Taylor at industry events or hanging out at her Rhode Island mansion! All-sister group Haim have remained pals ever since. They collaborated with Taylor on **'No Body, No Crime'**, and performed on the Eras Tour!

SELENA GOMEZ

Selena is Taylor's oldest celebrity mate. The pair first **met in 2005**! The former Disney girl has shared her admiration for Taylor on many occasions. "She has showed up for me in ways that I would never have expected ... she is **one of my best friends** in the world," Selena says.

JACK ANTONOFF

Taylor's **main co-writer** has become one of her closest companions. "I've seen her **change the music industry** first hand," says the man who helped pen **'Getaway Car'**, **'Cruel Summer'**, **'Anti-Hero'** and many more.

ABIGAIL ANDERSON BERARD

The red-headed school friend who featured in 'Fifteen' is still Taylor's pal now. After the release of *Folklore*, Taylor gifted her the official album cardigan. She showed her love for Abigail again by playing 'Fifteen' when the Eras Tour visited Nashville!

KATY PERRY

Katy is one of Taylor's most curious pals. For a long time, they didn't get on! But Katy sent Taylor an olive branch on the first night of the Reputation Tour. They confirmed their friendship in the **'You Need To Calm Down'** video. The two cuddled up with Katy in a burger costume and Tay dressed as a portion of chips!

ZOE KRAVITZ

Taylor and Zoe Kravitz helped each other get through the pandemic. "She was my pod," Zoe told GQ in 2020. "She was a very important part of being in London, just having a friend that I could see and that would make me home-cooked meals and dinner on my birthday."

GIGI HADID

Taylor performed **'Forever & Always'** for her friend Gigi when the Eras Tour stopped off in Philadelphia. She's one of many Taylor besties who appeared in the spectacular video for **'Bad Blood'**. Other Girl Squad members to feature included: Hailee Steinfeld, Cara Delevingne, Hayley Williams and Karlie Kloss!

EMMA STONE

The *La La Land* actress is a long-time friend of Taylor's and was spotted dancing joyously at the Eras Tour in Arizona. "To do three-and-a-half hours and perform 44 songs … **I've never seen anything like it**," Emma said.

MARISKA HARGITAY

Early in her career, Taylor described Mariska as **her idol** – so it's super cute that they've gone on to become great friends! Swift even **named her cat, Olivia Benson**, after one of Mariska's TV characters. In return, Mariska now has a **cat called Karma**!

1989

Out for a stroll in her new home, New York City, 2014.

WELCOME TO NEW YORK ...

Taylor's iconic *1989* album sold over 1.2 million copies in its first week alone! Inspired by her move to New York City in 2014, we begin the *1989* tale with 'Welcome to New York'. Exploring themes of love, heartbreak and becoming yourself, the country star's first true pop album was an instant success.

HATERS GONNA HATE

1989 tells a **new story** of Taylor's life. Hits such as **'Shake It Off'** and **'Clean'** were among the last songs to be written and have a clear 'I don't care what you think' vibe. As Taylor put it, they show "where I ended up mentally". She was **growing up** and coming into her own, **increasing in confidence** and, as she stated in the prologue to the album, "coming alive".

"I've learned how to shake things off."

From Taylor's 1989 Album Prologue

WILDEST DREAMS

Taylor put her heart into her songs – literally. She put the **sound of her heartbeat** into the song **'Wildest Dreams'**, earning an additional **instrumentalist credit** on the track. Beat that!

HERE TO STAY

You could say that *1989* showed us TS was here to stay – the album **changed her career forever**. She made it clear that she wasn't just sticking to her roots in country music, but she could **experiment** with a multitude of musical moods and genres. Swift was no longer just considered a country singer, she had officially made the **crossover to the pop world**.

STARBUCKS LOVERS?

We all know that iconic phrase from **'Blank Space'** that belongs in the **misheard lyrics** hall of fame. But even Taylor's mum thought it sounded like 'Starbucks lovers'! Time to give it another listen – what do you hear?

BACK TO THE BEGINNING

Pop never goes out of style! Drawing **inspo from the 1980s**, the decade in which she was born, Taylor was particularly inspired by electro-pop artists like **Peter Gabriel** and **Annie Lennox**.

Taylor dazzled in her sequin bomber jacket; her iconic look on the 1989 Tour, 2015. She paired the colourful jacket with a sparkly black crossover crop top and metallic blue skater skirt. Too cool for school!

13 ... TOP COLLABS

Taylor has buddied up with some of the most esteemed names in music – and a few unexpected ones, too!

London fans loved Taylor and Ed Sheeran performing 'Everything Has Changed' together at the 2013 Capital FM Summertime Ball.

1 ED SHEERAN

Ed wrote **'Everything Has Changed'** with Taylor in her back garden! They followed up with **'End Game'** on *Reputation* and **'Run'** on *Red (Taylor's Version)*. Oh, and a brilliant duetting remix of top Sheeran track **'The Joker and The Queen'**!

2 THE CHICKS

The Chicks (formerly the Dixie Chicks) were huge inspirations for Taylor's early country choruses. It must have been a pinch-me moment for our girl when they agreed to duet on **'Soon You'll Get Better'**.

3 FLORENCE + THE MACHINE

Taylor teams up with two massive artists on *The Tortured Poets Department*. Post Malone joins her on **'Fortnight'**, while **'Florida!!!'** features Florence + The Machine.

Florence loves a collab, having previously recorded with Dizzee Rascal!

4 THE NATIONAL

As well as helping to pen songs like **'Cardigan'** and **'Invisible String'**, **Aaron Dessner** is in a group called The National – and the full band teamed up with Taylor on *Evermore* track **'Coney Island'**.

5 HAIM

Some have joked that Taylor is the **fourth member** of sister act Haim! They've performed with her on the Eras Tour, teamed up on **'No Body, No Crime'**, and featured Tay on a remix of their song **'Gasoline'**.

6 ICE SPICE

One of Taylor's top traits is re-releasing a hot album track with a new vocal twist or fresh flavour. Ice Spice brought both to **'Karma'**! The song was nominated for Best Pop Duo/Group Performance at the 2024 **Grammy Awards**.

7 TIM McGRAW

Yes, he's more than just a song name! McGraw has been releasing **country albums** since 1993, and even sang **'Tim McGraw'** with Taylor when the Reputation Tour came to Nashville! Before that, they partnered on 2013 smash **'Highway Don't Care'**.

8 ZAYN

Swift linked up with former One Direction member Zayn on 2016 ballad **'I Don't Wanna Live Forever'**, scoring 25 million radio listens in its first week alone!

9 KENDRICK LAMAR

1989's cool co-write with rapper Lamar hoovered up the gold. **'Bad Blood'** won the **2014 Best Music Video Grammy** as well as **MTV Awards** for Video of the Year and Best Collaborations.

10 LANA DEL REY

Lana featured on **'Snow On The Beach'** – and revealed that Taylor initially wanted her to perform the entire track! **"She wanted me to sing the whole thing**, but if it ain't broke, don't fix it," Lana told Harper's Bazaar.

11 BON IVER

This indie-folk band is fronted by the incredible voice of **Justin Vernon**. He's teamed up with Taylor twice. **'Evermore'**, from *Evermore* (duh!) is good – but the duet fans remember most fondly is heartbreaking *Folklore* track **'Exile'**.

The 2019 Billboard Awards gave us a seriously sparkly live rendition of 'ME!'. No panic at this disco!

12 BRENDON URIE

A highlight of the *Miss Americana* documentary is going behind the scenes of Taylor working with someone new. It shows **Panic! At The Disco** frontman Brendon performing the vocals to **'ME!'**, as well as a sneak peek at how the video was made!

13 PHOEBE BRIDGERS

Up-and-coming songstress Phoebe opened the **Eras Tour** shows in Nashville and New Jersey, and teamed with T-Swift on **'Nothing New'**, from *Red (Taylor's Version)*.

REPUTATION

REVENGE IS SWEET

"I'm sorry. The old Taylor can't come to the phone right now. Why? Oh. 'Cause she's dead." If there's one T-Swift lyric which sums up her transformation from country-pop icon to the biggest superstar on earth, it's that interlude from 'Look What You Made Me Do'. *Reputation* came out in November 2017 and no musician has been able to keep up since.

The Reputation Tour kicked off with '...Ready For It?', while 'Delicate' and 'Dress' provided mid-set highlights!

A YEAR OFF

Usually Taylor takes roughly two years to write an album. For *Reputation*, **she took an extra 12 months** out of the spotlight, after being worn down by the media obsession with her private life. The resulting set of songs were laced with **anger and vengeance**. That's where the title comes from: restoring her reputation!

GETAWAY FOR THE SUMMER

Everyone loves TikTok phenomenon **'Cruel Summer'**, from the *Lover* album. But here's a special secret tip. Create a playlist with poppy *Reputation* track **'Getaway Car'** positioned directly before **'Cruel Summer'**. The electronic beats between those two tracks match perfectly!

SLITHERY FRIEND

One animal became a symbol for this album: the **snake**! It featured in official merch and the background of the Reputation Tour. Taylor explained why during a gig in Arizona: "A couple of years ago, **someone called me a snake** on social media and it caught on … I went through some times when I didn't know if I was going to get to do this anymore."

DELICATE DEVELOPMENT

Taylor wanted to keep the album **top secret**. Co-writer Jack Antonoff **disconnected his computer** from the internet while making it, so there was no way it could leak!

SO IT GOES …

Reputation's **song order** is genius. Early tracks like **'...Ready For It?'** and **'I Did Something Bad'** are aggressive and angry – but things get more chilled with **'Gorgeous'** and **'This Is Why We Can't Have Nice Things'**. It cleverly mirrors someone **getting furious, then calming down**!

MYSTERY VOCAL

Ever wondered whose voice says **'gorgeous'** at the start of that song? It's Ryan Reynolds and Blake Lively's daughter, James!

REPUTATION RECORDS

Reputation **sold two million copies in its first week**, proving Taylor's fans loved her more than ever. This was made even clearer as the Reputation Tour became the **highest-grossing tour** in American history. It made $266 million!

Taylor's outfit for the 2018 American Music Awards may be the most glam ever. She looked like a giant disco ball!

TOTALLY TAYLOR: AT HOME WITH TAYLOR

Taylor apparently has eight homes, across four American states! But what does she get up to when she isn't touring or recording? These are some of her happiest hobbies ...

Taylor's house in Rhode Island is called High Watch. It inspired 'The Last Great American Dynasty'!

BAKING

One of TayTay's favourite ways to wind down is by baking. Over the years she's shared plenty of her **home-made treats** on social media, including cupcakes and whoopie pies. Most delicious of all were **choc chip cookies** with M&M's embedded inside. Yum!

Rest assured Taylor's sugar cookies were even yummier than these ones!

TV WATCHING

Taylor loves some **chill out time** in front of the gogglebox while cuddling up with her three cats. Her fave shows include *Grey's Anatomy*, *CSI*, *Friends*, *The Office* and *Fuller House*.

BILLIARDS

T-Swift owns an incredible **loft apartment in New York**. As well as ten bathrooms and ten bedrooms, it has its own billiards room!

WORKING OUT

Another of Taylor's New York homes has **its own gym**, which is one of the main ways she perfected the Eras Tour! "Every day I would **run on the treadmill, singing the entire set list** out loud," she told *Time* magazine. "Fast for fast songs, and a jog or a fast walk for slow songs."

LISTENING TO MUSIC

Taylor doesn't just make amazing choruses – she's an avid listener, too! At the 2024 Grammy Awards she sang and danced along to **Olivia Rodrigo's** spectacular performance of 'Vampire'. Tay has even shared Spotify playlists of her fave tunes, featuring the likes of **Halsey, Kesha and Charli XCX**.

SNOW GLOBES

Growing up on a **Christmas tree farm** had a huge influence on Taylor. In the build up to the festive period, she likes to make snow globes with her friends. Earlier in her career she used to share them on Insta!

COLLECTING ANTIQUES

One of Taylor's favourite ways to spend her hard-earned cash is on antiques. She's been spotted shopping for old-school treasures in Nashville, Paris and the famous **Portobello Market in London**!

NEW LANGUAGES

When Taylor visits a country that speaks a different language, she respectfully tries to master some of the **local lingo**. "I always **try to adapt myself** a little bit by learning a few phrases," she told David Letterman in 2010. "When I'm in Japan I just speak in Japanese the entire show!"

TS shopping in Portobello Market. Its been one of London's coolest locations since 1863!

LOVER

TAYLOR GOES POP

T-Swift's break-up songs are a massive part of her DNA. So she really shook things up with her seventh album. It was all about being in love! The album came out in August 2019 and was supposed to lead to the massive Lover Fest tour. Sadly, the 2020 lockdown meant those plans had to be cancelled.

'Lover', 'ME!' and 'You Need To Calm Down' all got live outings at the iHeartRadio Jingle Ball in 2019.

HAPPY TRANSFORMATION

Lover's **bright and breezy sound** was the opposite of *Reputation*! If that album was about fighting back against her critics, then *Lover* **celebrated those who'd stood with her** all along. It meant massive bubblegum pop tunes like **'ME!'**, **'Cruel Summer'** and **'Paper Rings'**.

NORTHERN LINE

'London Boy' is about Taylor's longtime ex-love Joe Alwyn, who grew up in the city. The voice at the start is Idris Elba! Taylor and Joe are no longer together but the happy days of their relationship **inspired loads of songs** across *Lover*, *Folklore* and *Evermore*. He's also the guy she sang about in **'Gorgeous'**.

NOT SO CRUEL

Second track **'Cruel Summer'** shows just how devoted Taylor's followers can be. It wasn't initially released as a single, but fans yelled its greatness from the rooftops. **The song finally came out on its own in 2023**, four years later – and instantly became *Lover*'s **only number one!**

A FAMILY TALE

With **18 tracks**, *Lover* features **more songs than any other album** Taylor has released. Everyone knows **'I Forgot That You Existed'** and **'The Man'**, but the deeper cuts hit home too. For instance, **'Soon You'll Get Better'** is about her mum **Andrea's** battle with cancer.

TRACK NINETEEN

The album was almost even longer. Those who've watched *Miss Americana* will know the song **'Only The Young'**. It was also written for *Lover*, but it was held back to come out alongside the documentary in January 2020.

MOVIE INSPIRATION

Taylor did sneak one amazing break-up song onto the album. **'Death By A Thousand Cuts'** was inspired by Gina Rodriguez rom-com *Something Great*. "This song is my proof that I don't have to stop writing **songs about heartache** and misery – which for me is incredible news," Taylor joked during her NPR Tiny Desk Concert.

Like the *Lover* album, Tay went technicolour in a Rosa Bloom romper for the 2019 iHeart Radio Music Awards.

TOTALLY TAYLOR: CAT CREW

Taylor has always loved kittens and even appeared as cheeky Bombalurina in the movie *Cats*! Here's a closer look at her three closest feline pals ...

MEREDITH GREY

Meredith is a **Scottish Fold** who Taylor adopted in 2011. She's named after a *Grey's Anatomy* character played by **Ellen Pompeo**, who was one of many Taylor pals to appear in the video to 'Bad Blood'. Meredith made a video cameo herself in **'ME!'**, alongside her sister Olivia.

Breed Scottish Fold
Gender Female
Birthday 10 November 2010
Adopted October 2011

Taylor clearly had fun in her *Cats* role as Bombalurina!

Meredith looks understandably concerned as her 'parents', Taylor and Brendon Urie, argued in the video for 'ME!'. Someone give poor Meredith a cuddle!

OLIVIA BENSON

Taylor's second cat is another **Scottish Fold**, who joined T-Swift's furry family in 2014. Taylor sometimes calls her **Dibbles**. Olivia is also named after a TV character, from the show *Law and Order: SVU*, played by **Mariska Hargitay**. Olivia appeared in the video for **'Karma'**, with Taylor stretching out on her soft fur!

Breed Scottish Fold   **Gender** Female
Birthday 23 January 2014   **Adopted** June 2014

In November 2023, Mariska Hargitay named her new cat Karma, paying tribute to Taylor's song. They really vibe like that!

RICH KITTY

According to cats.com, Olivia Benson is the **third richest pet on the planet**! After appearing in ads for Diet Coke and Ned Sneakers, she's estimated to be **worth $97 million**. The only richer feline is Nala Cat, at $100 million. Top of the list is Gunther VI – a dog who used to be owned by Madonna and is worth $500 million!

BENJAMIN BUTTON

TayTay chose a different breed for her third cute kitty, who she calls **Benji** for short. He's a **Ragdoll**. Benjamin was adopted in 2019, after **appearing in the video for 'ME!'**. Taylor loved him so much she decided she couldn't live without him!

Breed Ragdoll   **Gender** Male
Birthday 18 December 2018   **Adopted** 2019

Brendon Urie gifts Taylor tiny kitten Bejamin in the 'ME!' video. Behind the scenes, Brendon commented that the cat's blue eyes were a similar hue to Swift's, joking that Benjamin must be her child!

AWARDS ADVENTURE

Olivia Benson and Benjamin Button got a surprise night out on the town in 2019. Taylor took them to the **Billboard Music Awards**! She used Instagram to share a photo of the pair meeting dance queen **Paula Abdul** on the red carpet. Here, Paula is holding Benjamin Button – lucky cat!

SNEAK PEEKS

All three of Taylor's kitties make regular appearances at her side. Olivia Benson is the cat on the bed during the mansion scenes in **'Blank Space'**. Meredith Grey was in the **'Midnights Mayhem With Me'** short where T-Swift announced **'Vigilante ****'**. And Benjamin Button appeared on the *Time* **magazine** cover when Taylor was named 2023 Person of the Year!

Of course Taylor looks purringly good in an Oscar de la Renta gown at the premiere of *Cats*.

QUEEN OF YOUR HEART

Olivia Benson won the **Nickelodeon Kids' Choice Award** for Favourite Celebrity Pet in 2023!

13 ... CRAZIEST HEADLINES

T-Swift is always in the news. Here are some of the most startling stories of her career!

1

"Taylor Swift announces new album during Grammy win."

The craziest Taylor news of 2024 happened as early as February, with *People* using this headline. Taylor stunned the world when collecting her award for **Best Pop Album**, by announcing her long-awaited eleventh album, ***The Tortured Poets Department***!

2

"Icon. Feminist. Rebel."

A special *Queens of Pop* issue dedicated to Taylor, after her triumphant *Reputation* comeback.

3

"Catitude? Meredith is out of control!"

Taylor released two magazines to tie in with *Reputation* and the back covers were made to look like a tabloid, with hilarious headlines like this one!

4

"Sunday night Taylor made for Glastonbury."

The Glastonbury Free Press announces that she will headline the famous festival in 2020. Sadly, **lockdown** meant the event never happened.

5

"Taylor Swift's 'All You Had To Do Was Stay' is criminally underrated."

Time magazine wrote a whole story in defence of one track from *1989*. Here's the thing: they're right!

6

"Why we love Taylor Swift (and why you should too)."

Country Weekly goes big on TayTay back in 2010. How right they were about the part in brackets!

Taylor popped flowers in her hair to look radiant at the Time 100 Gala in 2019.

7

"Taylor Swift reveals weird but sweet reason she might stare at you at her concerts."

The Mirror revealed this in 2023, but of course her explanation was innocent: **"If you see me staring at you, it's just because I'm actively trying to memorise your faces."** Lush!

8

"Even Taylor Swift thought it was funny that she had to run offstage."

Vanity Fair reports on a mishap on the Eras Tour. A **trapdoor** failed to open, so Taylor sprinted offstage past her dancers instead. Fans joked that the move was called **'Run (Taylor's Version)'**!

9

"Taylor Swift's peculiar request to *Time* when she was named Person of the Year for 2023."

Inspired by a 1970s book called *Cat People*, she asked if **Benjamin Button** could appear on the cover with her! The editors of course said 'yes'.

10

"Newspaper chain hiring Beyonce and Swift reporters."

CNN reveals the staggering news that **USA Today** is creating two new jobs, to report on nothing other than Beyoncé and Taylor Swift.

11

"This feels like a new beginning."

Taylor shows the video for **'You Need To Calm Down'** to *Vogue*, eight days before unleashing it on the world!

12

"Who is Olivia's real father?"

Another hilarious Taylor back cover headline from the magazines released to tie in with **Reputation**. She clearly has a huge sense of fun when it comes to her kitties!

13

"Taylor Swift rules the world and we are her loyal subjects."

The October 2015 edition of *GQ* magazine offers the most accurate headline in journalism history. Hail queen Taylor!

Taylor rocked the glamorous pink fluffy coat, bejewelled sunnies and heart earrings in the 'You Need To Calm Down' video!

FOLKLORE

A QUARANTINE TREAT

The year 2020 changed the course of Taylor's career. Instead of performing the Lover Fest tour and headlining Glastonbury, she was holed up inside, with just her cats for company. It led to an astonishing announcement on 23 July. TayTay had been working on a secret album called *Folklore* – and it was being released at midnight!

Taylor performed *Folklore* at Long Pond Studio, along with co-writers Jack Antonoff and Aaron Dessner. The trio picked up the Album of the Year Grammy in 2021!

JULY JOY

Taylor's announcement came on Instagram and **stunned** even the most avid fan. "Most of the things I had planned this summer didn't end up happening, but there is **something I hadn't planned on** that DID happen," she wrote. "And that thing is my 8th studio album, *Folklore*".

FIRST AND LAST

'My Tears Ricochet' was the first song penned for *Folklore*, and inspired by the divorce storyline in 2019 film *Marriage Story*. **'The 1'** and **'Hoax'** were the final two songs Taylor wrote, and finished just hours apart!

ACROSS THE NATION

Taylor worked remotely with two brilliant musicians: long-time collaborator **Jack Antonoff**, and The National guitarist **Aaron Dessner**. With those two guys based in New York while Taylor was in Los Angeles, *Folklore* was less a country album – and more a **cross-country album**!

A MILLION LITTLE TIMES

'Illicit Affairs' followed in the footsteps of **'Cruel Summer'** by becoming a **TikTok phenomenon**. Taylor changed the arrangement for the Eras Tour, and it's now unofficially known and worshipped as **'Illicit Affairs (Angry Version)'**!

INVISIBLE STRING

It was a sombre year for families around the world. *Folklore*'s **gentle vibe** felt in tune with that mood, yet uplifting at the same time. Haunting pianos, thoughtful string arrangements and poetic lyrics added to Taylor's **most mellow album yet**.

BETTY, JAMES & AUGUSTINE

One of the main reasons Swift fans adore *Folklore* is because of the **love triangle** between three fictional teenage characters. **'Cardigan'**, **'Betty'** and **'August'** tell the tale from each of the trio's perspectives. Fans have spent years deciphering exactly what the lyrics mean!

MYSTERY SCRIBE

Three singles were released from *Folklore*: **'Cardigan'** (which became her sixth number one), **'Exile'** and **'Betty'**. The latter pair featured a **mysterious songwriting partner**, William Bowery. This was a pretend name for Taylor's boyfriend at the time, Joe Alwyn!

Little did anyone know what 2020 had in store when Taylor debuted *Miss Americana* at January's Sundance Film Festival.

53

TOTALLY TAYLOR: I ♥ T.S.

Taylor's legion of fans are famously loyal and dedicated. These are some of the ways they show their devotion ...

INTERNET BREAKING

The launch of the **Eras Tour** was so popular that it broke sales site Ticketmaster! **14 million people** tried to buy tickets for the US dates alone, with 2 million lucky enough to get one. It was the most tickets Ticketmaster had ever sold for a single artist in one day.

EASTER EGG HUNTING

TS fans love analysing her videos, interviews and social media posts for Easter eggs. Taylor loves coming up with them just as much! "We have a PDF file for the Easter eggs in this video," she joked about '**Bejeweled**', "because there are so many that we could not keep track." They included an appearance from **Haim**, a portrait featuring her cats and *Speak Now* hairpins!

A selfie with Taylor is the ultimate goal for any true fan!

WRISTBAND EXCHANGING

"So, make the **friendship bracelets**, take the moment and taste it." That one line from '**You're On Your Own, Kid**' started a trend that continued throughout the Eras Tour, with fans making their own wristbands to share. Even celebs such as Jennifer Lawrence, Nicole Kidman and Channing Tatum got involved!

Swapping friendship bracelets makes the Eras Tour a truly special night.

TAYLOR SWIFT
THE ERAS TOUR

GLENDALE, AZ
LAS VEGAS, NV
ARLINGTON, TX
TAMPA, FL
HOUSTON, TX
ATLANTA, GA
NASHVILLE, TN
PHILADELPHIA, PA
FOXBOROUGH, MA
EAST RUTHERFORD, NJ

CHICAGO, IL
DETROIT, MI
PITTSBURGH, PA
MINNEAPOLIS, MN
CINCINNATI, OH
KANSAS CITY, MO
DENVER, CO
SEATTLE, WA
SANTA CLARA, CA
LOS ANGELES, CA

2 0 2 3

Most fans arrived at the Eras Tour hours in advance, to savour the atmosphere.

VINYL COLLECTING

Old school records have made a comeback, and fans' attempts to collect them all has meant some now fetch crazy prices. Taylor released a **heart-shaped** *City of Lover* **vinyl** with four tracks recorded at her one-off Paris gig in 2019. Each copy is worth over £500!

TAYLOR'S VERSION BUYING

No other artist has ever set about **re-recording** their original albums then hoping fans buy them for a second time. But Taylor's fanbase have backed the approach with total dedication! *Fearless (Taylor's Version)* shot to **number one** in nine different countries, while *1989 (Taylor's Version)* sold a mind-blowing **3.5 million copies** in a single week!

TAYLOR GATING

Those who couldn't get tickets for the Eras Tour made sure they didn't miss out – by **dancing in the carpark outside the stadiums** instead! The trend became known as 'Taylor Gating'. It's a play on words from Tailgating, when sports fans meet up for BBQs before big events. Around **20,000** joined in when Taylor played Philadelphia!

Australian fans trading bracelets at the Eras Tour in Melbourne. A really g'day!

EVERMORE

A LITTLE MORE FOLKLORE

Taylor's ninth album came out just five months after *Folklore*, in December 2020, and is considered its little sister. *Evermore* continued the theme of low-key, folky tunes with sombre or mellow elements. 11 of the 15 tracks were penned with *Folklore* co-writer Aaron Dessner, while Bon Iver returned on the final song – also called 'Evermore'!

Aaron Dessner tracks on Evermore include 'Willow', 'Dorothea' and 'Long Story Short'.

ANOTHER RECORD

Evermore was one of 2020's **top ten selling albums** – even though it was only available for the last two weeks of the year! It went to **number one** at the same time as *Folklore* being number three. This made Taylor the first woman ever to have **two albums in the top three** at once!

THE PERFECT SETTING

Have you watched **The Long Pond Studio Sessions** yet? Then you'll understand why *Evermore* is such a relaxing, calm record. It was recorded at Long Pond! It's a beautiful barn owned by **Aaron Dessner**, **surrounded by nature** – with three bedrooms upstairs, for a perfect night's sleep.

GRANDMOTHER LOVE

'Marjorie' is about Taylor's grandma, Marjorie Finlay. She was an **opera singer** who won a TV talent contest on *Music With the Girls* in 1950! Some of Marjorie's opera recordings can be heard in the background of the song.

EXPENSIVE JUMPER

The official *Evermore* **cardigan** is one of the **rarest pieces of Taylor merch** ever made. It's a boxy grey knit sweater with green stars on the arms. One was listed on eBay at the end of 2023 – and sold for £908!

DOUBLE DUTY

The last days of making *Evermore* overlapped with Taylor's work on *Fearless (Taylor's Version)*. She even recorded **'Happiness'** on the exact same day as **'You Belong With Me (Taylor's Version)'**.

SHE DID IT

A Billboard fan vote named **'No Body, No Crime'** the best song on the album. 18% of fans chose it as their number one, ahead of **'Champagne Problems'** (15%) and **'Willow'** (13%).

A CHRISTMAS CRACKER

This thoughtful, comforting album came in time for Christmas in 2020, during the **pandemic**. "This season will be a lonely one for most of us and if there are any of you out there who turn to music to cope with missing loved ones the way I do, **this is for you**," Taylor wrote on social media to announce *Evermore*.

Lockdown stopped Taylor performing live, but she was honoured with the Global Icon Award at the 2021 Brit Awards!

TOTALLY TAYLOR: COOLEST CONCERTS

T-Swift has crammed some phenomenal one-off shows into her amazing career. If you were at any of these, treasure the memory for life!

CITY OF LOVER, 2019

The *Lover* album never got a tour due to the world being in lockdown shortly after its release – which made this one-off gig even more special. Taylor performed for **2,000 fans** at the **Olympia theatre in Paris**, and included a magical six-song acoustic section featuring new songs like **'The Man'** and **'Cornelia Street'**.

BLUEBIRD CAFE, 2018

Before she got her first record deal, Taylor would perform in a **90-seat Nashville club** called the Bluebird Cafe. It's always been special to her, so over a decade later she went back to play **'Better Man'** with country favourite **Craig Wiseman**. She originally wrote the song for group Little Big Town, but it later appeared on *Red (Taylor's Version)*.

THE LONG POND STUDIO SESSIONS, 2020

What do you do when no one is allowed out to watch concerts? Perform your lockdown album in a beautiful barn, then **broadcast it to the world**! Taylor teamed up with co-writers Jack Antonoff and Aaron Dessner for this incredible rendition of *Folklore*. **'August'**, **'Betty'** and **'This Is Me Trying'** are especially memorable.

ERAS TOUR (PHILADELPHIA), 2023

The Eras Tour became so massive that last-minute tickets sold for thousands of pounds. That meant many couldn't afford to go. Instead, they parked outside the venue for a **giant singalong**! Thousands danced along to the entire show in Philadelphia and were rewarded with two old favourites as secret songs: **'Forever & Always'** and **'This Love'**!

AMERICAN MUSIC AWARDS, 2019

A truly iconic performance. Taylor won **Artist of the Decade** shortly after having her entire back catalogue of albums sold off by her **old record company**. That meant she was no longer officially allowed to perform songs like **'Love Story'** or **'Blank Space'** live! So that's exactly what she did, busting out a defiant medley which included those tracks alongside new ones from *Lover*.

TINY DESK CONCERT, 2019

Tiny Desk is a series of concerts recorded behind a **cluttered desk** in Washington, DC! Surrounded by books and records, a small number of fans get to watch each show. **300** crammed in to watch Taylor perform four perfect songs: **'The Man'**, **'Lover'**, **'Death By A Thousand Cuts'** and **'All Too Well'**.

13 ... BEST MUSIC VIDEOS

TayTay's tunes are faultless and her vids complete the perfect package. Remember these classics?

Dylan O'Brien and Sadie Sink looking so sweet together – we're not crying.

1 ALL TOO WELL: THE SHORT FILM

Taylor's first short film is everything fans hoped for. The 15-minute clip starring **Dylan O'Brien** from *Teen Wolf* and *Stranger Things* favourite **Sadie Sink** visualises the song's heartbreaking tale perfectly. The red scarf – OMG!

2 LOVE STORY

Filmed at Castle Gwynn in Tennessee and featuring model Justin Gaston, this clip has a soft spot in every Swift fan's brain. The **ballroom scene** stars 20 dancers from a local university, and fresh-faced Taylor learned the moves **just 15 minutes before filming**.

3 BAD BLOOD

This Taylor vid was quite literally **explosive**! It could be an **action film** in its own right, with plenty of **special effects** and a deadly girl squad to back up our fierce protagonist.

Taylor looked fiery in 'Bad Blood' with her bold eyeliner and deep red hair.

4 WE ARE NEVER EVER GETTING BACK TOGETHER

This video marked Taylor's transformation **from country gal to pop songstress**. She ushered in the *Red* era with **lipstick** of the same colour, and also showed off her longer bangs for the first time. This is exhausting. Not!

5 LOOK WHAT YOU MADE ME DO

Taylor took an extra year off before unleashing the '**Look What You Made Me Do**' video, relaunching herself to the world as a **zombie**! Those opening scenes are the scariest of her career, but very cool, too.

6 CRAZIER

Never heard of this one? It's from *Hannah Montana: The Movie*, in which Taylor played herself! It's definitely worth a retro watch as a reminder of both her and **Miley Cyrus'** early days.

7 CARDIGAN

The *Folklore* era got underway in head-turning fashion as Taylor played her **piano in a cabin**, before clinging to it on the **open ocean**. It's utterly beautiful – but boy does that water look freezing!

YOU NEED TO CALM DOWN

Taylor brought all the colour and Easter eggs for this **LGBTQ+ anthem**. Taylor spends some quality time **dolled up in her blow-up pool**, before hanging out with a long list of **famous faces** round a trailer park!

8

Anyone would calm down in a pool with a pink furry coat, bikini and heels on!

9 MEAN

The only video of Taylor playing a **banjo** with a loose side braid. Enough said!

This guy was added to Taylor's long list of ex-lovers in the video for 'Blank Space'!

10 BLANK SPACE

Big-budget video showcasing the rise and fall of a mansion-owning couple, with Taylor looking at her swankiest – and a bonus appearance from **pet cat Olivia**!

11 YOU BELONG WITH ME

The first proof that Taylor could act out multiple characters in one video. She played both the **specs-wearing protagonist** and the brunette bad girl in this long-time fan favourite!

12 SHAKE IT OFF

The best known Taylor video of them all, with **3.4 billion YouTube views**. It features loads of cool pop culture references, including Daft Punk, ballet movie *Black Swan* and Miley Cyrus' love of twerking!

13 THE MAN

Written by Taylor Swift, directed by Taylor Swift and featuring Taylor Swift as … the man. Obvs!

MIDNIGHTS

WAKING UP TO A NEW SOUND

Album number ten was Taylor's take on all the things that keep us awake at night! *Midnights* heralded a big departure from *Folklore* and *Evermore*, with lots of electronics and even some hip hop elements. The album dropped in October 2022 and spawned three singles: 'Anti-Hero', 'Lavender Haze' and 'Karma'.

Taylor tied the record for most wins in one night at the VMAs in 2023, with nine!

BIG GIG

The build towards the album began in July 2022, six months before release. Taylor made a **shock appearance** onstage during a **Haim gig** in London. It was her first live performance in three years! They played an amazing mash-up of **'Love Story'** and Haim song **'Gasoline'**.

EIGHT IS GREAT

'Anti-Hero' was released as a single on the same day that the album came out. It spent **eight weeks** at **number one** on the Billboard Hot 100, making it Taylor's **longest run at the top of the charts yet**!

CATCHING REYS

Big-name collabs were officially back for *Midnights*! **Lana Del Rey** guested on **'Snow On The Beach'**, while **Zoe Kravitz** co-wrote **'Lavender Haze'**. Oh, and **Ice Spice** linked up with Taylor for the single version of **'Karma'**.

LYRICAL RAINBOW

Midnights features more references to **colour** than any other Taylor album. There are **40 mentions** in total! These include scarlet on **'Maroon'**, crimson on **'The Great War'** and Aurora Borealis green in **'Snow On The Beach'**!

PURPLE REIGN

Six differently coloured versions of *Midnights* were released on **vinyl**! They come in lavender, jade green, moonstone blue, mahogany, blood moon and love potion purple. That last one is the rarest, and worth around £60.

ALL-TAY TOP TEN

Midnights' songs made Taylor the **first ever artist to occupy all Billboard Top 10 spots** in one week! Number one was **'Anti-Hero'**, followed by **'Lavender Haze'**, **'Maroon'**, **'Snow On The Beach'**, **'Midnight Rain'**, **'Bejeweled'**, **'Question...?'**, **'You're On Your Own, Kid'**, **'Karma'** and **'Vigilante ****'**.

KARMIC CHEER

Taylor told Apple Music that she is especially **proud of 'Karma'**: "It is written from a perspective of feeling, like, really **happy** … We can't just be beating ourselves up all the time."

GOOD QUESTION

'Question...?' might have a simple melody, but it's very clever beneath the surface. It starts off with a sample of *1989* single **'Out Of The Woods'** – while Jack Antonoff's sister Rachel, and Taylor's brother Austin, provide crowd noises!

Midnights famously makes up the finale of the Eras Tour. Highlights include 'Anti-Hero', 'Mastermind' and 'Karma'!

63

13 ... BEST VIDEO CAMEOS

Some of the biggest names in entertainment have popped up in Taylor's promo clips over the years!

1 YOU NEED TO CALM DOWN

The first single from *Lover* features allllll the crazy antics. **Adam Lambert** tattoos **Ellen DeGeneres**, **Jesse Tyler Ferguson** (Mitch from *Modern Family*) gets married, the cast of **Queer Eye** come for tea, and **Katy Perry** and T-Swift hug while dressed up as a burger and fries!

2 ME!

Panic! At The Disco frontman **Brendon Urie** guests in this video, which plays off classic musicals like *Mary Poppins*. The best bit is when he and Tay dance in the street amid a flood of **colourful paint**.

3 BAD BLOOD

The video which introduced the world to Taylor's **Girl Squad**. It features loads of her pals, with badass alter-egos. Lena Dunham becomes Lucky Fiori, Cara Delevingne is Mother Chucker and modelling legend Cindy Crawford stars as **Headmistress**!

4 TEARDROPS ON MY GUITAR

Love interest Drew is played by **Tyler Hilton** in this single from first album *Taylor Swift*. Tyler also had an important role in a bigger musical movie. He played Elvis Presley in *Walk The Line*, which profiles the life of country icon Johnny Cash.

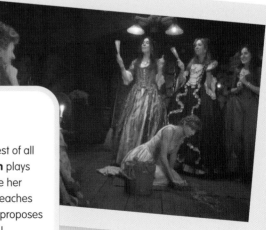

5 BEJEWELED

Many fans reckon this is the coolest of all the *Midnights* videos. **Laura Dern** plays Taylor's evil stepmother, **Haim** are her stepsisters and **Dita Von Teese** teaches her a routine. Also, Jack Antonoff proposes to Taylor – but sadly gets ghosted!

6 ANTI-HERO

Comedians John Early and Mike Birbiglia appear alongside Mary Elizabeth Ellis from *It's Always Sunny In Philadelphia*. They're guests at **Taylor's pretend funeral**, where she leaves everything to her cats!

7 END GAME

Taylor kicks this one off partying on a boat with rapper **Future** in Miami. She's then joined by **Ed Sheeran** for some chill out time in a Tokyo karaoke bar, before heading to London for a house party with other pals. Phew!

8 I DON'T WANNA LIVE FOREVER

Taylor Swift and **Zayn Malik**. Could this be the dreamiest couple in a video, ever?

9 YOU BELONG WITH ME

Taylor met actor **Lucas Till** while filming her appearance in *The Hannah Montana Movie*. It led to him playing the cute guy next door in this beloved vid!

10 WILDEST DREAMS

The video for this romantic single from the *1989* album is a treat. Tay looks delightful with **jet-black hair** on the set of a pretend movie in **Africa**, where **Scott Eastwood** from *Wrath of Man* portrays fictional co-star Robert Kingsley.

11 I KNEW YOU WERE TROUBLE

Reeve Carney plays Taylor's love interest in this LA-based clip. He's another actor with a musical background, having once played guitar for blues rocker Jonny Lang.

12 KARMA

Ice Spice brought a fresh new rap to the video for this *Midnights* banger, racking up **53 million YouTube views** in just eight months! The pair looked like a magical, sparkly dream in the video.

13 I BET YOU THINK ABOUT ME

Miles Teller has scored a ton of top movie roles, including Reed Richards in *Fantastic Four*. He was persuaded to appear in this video alongside real-life wife **Keleigh Sperry Teller** – as Taylor crashes their wedding day!

TOTALLY TAYLOR: ONE DAY ON THE ERAS TOUR

Wondering what it's like to actually experience the Eras Tour? Taylor superfan Bee flew all the way from London to watch Taylor live in Tampa!

2pm GETTING READY

"An early start as my hotel is three miles from the stadium. The ones nearby were more than £2,000 per night! I'm wearing **heart-shaped shades**, a 'Cruel Summer' tee and the lobby is packed with **fans** waiting for taxis. A sign by the front desk says: 'Ready For It?' Yes!"

3pm TAYGATE TIME

"I get dropped off at a venue 20 minutes' walk from the stadium for an unofficial **'TayGate'**. It's packed with fans of all ages, and there are drinks with names like 'Feeling 22' and 'Out of the Woods'. The owners have set up displays to look like album covers, which you and your friends can pose in front of. Very cool!"

4:30pm QUEUE BELONG WITH ME

"Arrive at the concert venue. So. Many. People! Raymond James Stadium holds **75,000** and most of them are already here, queueing to get in! But security are friendly and it only takes 20 minutes before I'm heading up the escalator into the **massive arena**. Waaaaa!"

4:50pm BRACELET SWAPPING

"A lovely fellow Swiftie stops me to swap **friendship bracelets**! It's a trend started by the song, **'You're On Your Own, Kid'**. I look around and everyone is doing it! She gives me one which spells out 'Karma', while mine to her says 'LWYMMD'. Can you work out the song?"

5:30pm BEABADOOBEE BEATS

"The queues for **merch** are crazy! So I pop to my seat for support acts Beabadoobee and Gayle, who are both toe-tappingly great. Towards the end of Gayle's set I find a merch queue that isn't too busy and finally snag a cream **'Eras Tour' T-shirt**. It's $45 – which is around £36 – but a priceless souvenir!"

7:55pm MISS AMERICANA

"Dancers carrying **pink umbrellas** move out onto the walkway, which stretches across half the stadium. They lift their umbrellas and … it's Taaaaaaylor! She leaps straight into **'Miss Americana & The Heartbreak Prince'**, followed by **'Cruel Summer'**. Everyone sings, dances, screams or tries to do all three at once!"

9pm DASH TO THE DOOR

"There's only one problem with Taylor's epic set. **Our queen doesn't do intervals!** That means sacrificing a song to get food or drink, or visit the loo! I miss **'Tolerate It'**, but an explosive rendition of **'...Ready For It?'** means there's no time to dwell."

11:15pm KARMA CLOSER

"After over **three hours, 44 songs and 16 costume changes**, the last notes of **'Karma'** fade away and a huge **fireworks show** takes over the night sky. **'Illicit Affairs'** was unbelievable, **'Style'** rocked the stadium and we all shook it off to **'Shake It Off'**. I've had goosebumps for the last 12,000 seconds. **Greatest gig ever!**"

THE TORTURED POETS DEPARTMENT

ELEVENTH HEAVEN IS HERE

Taylor stunned the watching world yet again at the 2024 Grammy Awards. After *Midnights* won the trophy for Best Pop Vocal Album, she announced her eleventh long-player: *The Tortured Poets Department*! It was a truly triumphant night, as she later collected the overall Best Album award, too.

Taylor's Grammys announcement sent social media into a meltdown.

MACHINE LEARNING

The Tortured Poets Department sees two new collaborators added to Taylor's ever-growing list of musical partnerships! 'Better Now' rapper **Post Malone** teams up with Tay on opening track **'Fortnight'**, while **'Florida!!!'** features none other than **Florence + The Machine**.

FALSE REPUTATION

Taylor fooled even the most dedicated fans with the **shock album announcement**. On the day of the Grammys she **made all her social media profile pictures black-and-white**, and everyone predicted the long-awaited reveal of *Reputation (Taylor's Version)*.

> *"I had this plan in my head and I told my friends ... but I hadn't really told many other people."*
>
> Taylor said this after her big Grammy reveal. She explained that she thought, *"'OK, so if I'm lucky enough to win one thing tonight, I'm just going to do it. I'm just going to announce my new album'."*

ENGLISH INSPIRATION

The album came out in April 2024, with 16 tracks in total and an understandable **break-up theme**, following Taylor's split with London boy Joe Alwyn. That explains track titles like **'So Long, London'** and **'My Boy Only Breaks His Favorite Toys'**.

HEARTBREAK ANTHEM

Taylor always makes **track five** of each album the most vulnerable song, such as **'All Too Well'** on *Red*. So the placement of **'So Long, London'** was a very deliberate choice!

DISC CHASING

The first **deluxe edition CD** of *The Tortured Poets Department* sold out within two hours! It includes a patch for bonus track **'The Manuscript'**. Taylor soon announced alternative versions, with different bonus tracks: **'The Bolter'**, **'The Albatross'** and **'The Black Dog'**.

Shortly before the album reveal, Taylor wowed the world in a green Gucci dress at the Golden Globes.

CREDITS

Front Cover: PICTURES: Alamy Images, Raj Valley

5: PICTURE: Alamy Images, MediaPunch Inc

6-7: PICTURES: Shutterstock, Press Line Photos / Alamy Images, Sipa US / Shutterstock, landmarkmedia / Shutterstock, DFree

8-9: PICTURES: Alamy Images, UPI / Shutterstock, Everett Collection / Alamy Images, WENN Rights Ltd

10-11: PICTURES: Alamy Images, Abaca Press / Shutterstock, s_bukley / Shutterstock, Everett Collection / Alamy Images, Sipa US / Alamy Images, ZUMA Press, Inc. / Shutterstock, Brian Friedman

12-13: WORDS: Genius.com: Taylor Swift, lyrics to 'All Too Well (10 Minute Version)' from *Red (Taylor's Version)*
PICTURES: Alamy Images, Shanna Madison / Shutterstock, melissamn / Shutterstock, a katz

14-15: WORDS: Ew.com: Chris Willman
PICTURES: Alamy Images, AFF / Shutterstock, Featureflash Photo Agency

16-17: PICTURES: Shutterstock, Everett Collection / Alamy Images, WENN Rights Ltd

18-19: PICTURES: Shutterstock, Kathy Hutchins / Shutterstock, Jaguar PS / Alamy Images, AFF / Shutterstock, Featureflash Photo Agency / Shutterstock, s_bukley / Alamy Images, AFF

20-21: WORDS: Time.com: Taylor Swift
PICTURES: Alamy Images, Sayre Berman / Shutterstock, Everett Collection

22-23: WORDS: Bbc.co.uk: Mark Savage, Soundslikenashville.com: Lauren Hostelley
PICTURES: Shutterstock, s_bukley / Alamy Images, UPI

24-25: PICTURES: Shutterstock, Ovidiu Hrubaru / Shutterstock, Tinseltown / Shutterstock, DFree / Shutterstock, FashionStock.com / Alamy Images, Abaca Press / Alamy Images, PA Images

26-27: WORDS: Songwriteruniverse.com: Bill Conger, Ew.com: Tanner Stransky
PICTURES: Shutterstock, Debby Wong / Alamy Images, WENN Rights Ltd

28-29: PICTURES: Alamy Images, Sayre Berman / Alamy Images, ZUMA Press, Inc.

30-31: PICTURES: Shutterstock, s_bukley / Shutterstock, Tinseltown / Alamy Images, PA Images / Shutterstock, Ovidiu Hrubaru / Shutterstock, Kathy Hutchins / Alamy Images, Australian Associated Press

32-33: WORDS: Eu.usatoday.com: Brian Mansfield
PICTURES: Shutterstock, FashionStock.com / Shutterstock, Featureflash Photo Agency

34-35: WORDS: Teenvogue.com: Naomi Nevitt, Time.com: Sam Lansky, Taylorswiftsongs2.blogspot.com, Nme.com: Alex Gallagher, Bustle.com: Kadeen Griffiths, *Lover* Deluxe Album Journal Version 1: Taylor Swift, Genius.com: Taylor Swift, *Fearless* Album Prologue, Elle.com: Taylor Swift
PICTURES: Shutterstock, Jamie Lamor Thompson / Alamy Images, EXImages / Shutterstock, Everett Collection / Alamy Images, PA Images

36-37: WORDS: Wsj.com: Derek Blasberg, Nme.com: Nick Reilly, Vanityfair.com: Paul Chi, Gq.com: Gabriella Paiella
PICTURES: Shutterstock, Kathy Hutchins / Shutterstock, Tinseltown / Alamy Images, WENN Rights Ltd

38-39: WORDS: Elle.com: Tavi Gevinson, Genius.com: Taylor Swift, *1989* Album Prologue, Buzzfeed.com: Sheridan Watson
PICTURES: Alamy Images, WENN Rights Ltd / Alamy Images, Sam Kovak

40-41: WORDS: Rollingstone.com: Tomás Mier
PICTURES: Alamy Images, Suzan Moore / Shutterstock, Christian Bertrand / Alamy Images, PictureLux/The Hollywood Archive

42-43: WORDS: Harpersbazaar.com: Erica Gonzales
PICTURES: Alamy Images, Australian Associated Press / Shutterstock, Featureflash Photo Agency

44-45: WORDS: Time.com: Sam Lansky, Taylor Swift: interview with David Letterman, 26th October 2010
PICTURES: Shutterstock, Carol Ann Mossa / Alamy Images, WENN Rights Ltd / Shutterstock, Hanna Summer / Shutterstock, anitnov

46-47: WORDS: Bbc.co.uk: Mark Savage
PICTURES: Shutterstock, Brian Friedman / Shutterstock, DFree

48-49: PICTURES: Alamy, Pictorial Press Ltd / YouTube, Taylor Swift, 'ME! ft. Brendon Urie' music video / YouTube, Taylor Swift, 'Karma ft. Ice Spice' music video / YouTube, Taylor Swift, 'ME! Behind The Scenes: The Story of Benjamin Button' video / Instagram, Taylor Swift / Alamy Images, WENN Rights Ltd / Shutterstock, J0v43 / Shutterstock, Drekhann

50-51: WORDS: People.com: Kirsty Hatcher, Queens of Pop Magazine, Special Issue 2019/20 / Taylor Swift, Reputation Magazines Volumes 1 & 2, 10th November 2017 / Glastonbury festivals.co.uk, Time.com: Rachel Sonis, Country Weekly Magazine, November 2010, Mirror.co.uk: Mollie Quirk, Vanityfair.com: Kase Wickman, Marca.com, CNN International News Report, 15th September 2023 / Huffingtonpost.co.uk: Cavan Sieczkowski
PICTURES: Alamy Images, UPI / YouTube, Taylor Swift, 'You Need To Calm Down' music video

52-53: WORDS: Taylorswift.tumblr.com: Taylor Swift
PICTURES: YouTube, Taylor Swift, 'exile (folklore: the long pond studio sessions | Disney+) ft. Bon Iver' video / Alamy Images, AFF

54-55: WORDS: Ew.com: Emlyn Travis
PICTURES: Shutterstock, Graham Drew Photography / Shutterstock, Featureflash Photo Agency / Alamy Images, Australian Associated Press / Shutterstock, EQRoy

56-57: PICTURES: Alamy Images, ZUMA Press, Inc. / Alamy Images, PA Images

58-59: PICTURES: YouTube, ABC, Taylor Swift, City of Lover Concert, 17th May 2019 / Alamy Images, Everett Collection Inc. / YouTube, imusic, Taylor Swift, 'the 1', Folklore: The Long Pond Studio Sessions, 25th November 2020 / Alamy Images, Raj Valley / Alamy Images, Xavier Collin / YouTube, NPR Music, Taylor Swift, Tiny Desk Concert, 16th October 2019

60-61: PICTURES: YouTube, Taylor Swift, 'All Too Well: The Short Film' music video, 'Bad Blood ft. Kendrick Lamar' music video, 'You Need To Calm Down' music video and 'Blank Space' music video

62-63: WORDS: Digital.abcaudio.com: Megan Stone
PICTURES: Alamy Images, UPI / Alamy Images, Australian Associated Press

64-65: PICTURES: YouTube, Taylor Swift, 'You Need To Calm Down' music video, 'Bad Blood ft. Kendrick Lamar' music video, 'Bejeweled' music video, 'Wildest Dreams' music video and 'Karma ft. Ice Spice' music video

66-67: PICTURES: Ben Wilson

68-69: WORDS: Bustle.com: Sam Ramsden
PICTURES: Getty Images, Monica Schipper / Alamy Images, Imago